MW00443870

CANNOLI CAN

CAN I CAN

ISBN 978-1-68570-631-9 (hardcover)
ISBN 978-1-68570-630-2 (digital)

Christian Faith Publishing
832 Park Avenue
Meadville, PA 16335
www.christianfaithpublishing.com

Printed in the United States of America

CaNNOLI CaN

Takes on Kindergarten

Emily Jennings Dito

Hi, everybody! My name is Cannoli, and I am five years old. My mom and my dad have been preparing me for a big, so-called life-changing event. It's called school. Better yet, it's called kindergarten. I can do it. I think.

Well, I have a secret that I need to share. I'm nervous to go to school. I tell Mom and Dad, and this is what they say, "There's no need to be nervous. You're going to love it, and you'll make so many new friends. You can do anything, Cannoli! You can."

I start thinking to myself, *I can't count by twos or tie my shoes and coloring in the lines, well, yeah right! I can't cut, I can't glue, and I certainly can't write.*

Then I think about all the things I can do, and boy, are there a lot. I can water the plants, I can do a fun dance, and I can tell my left from my right. Maybe Mom and Dad are onto something. You can do anything, Cannoli. You can.

Mom helps me lay out my outfit, and then she reads me a bedtime story. Then Dad tucks me in tight and turns off the light, and I lie there, thinking, *Cannoli, you can!*

I fall asleep by counting sheep, and then just like that, the sun begins to rise.

The dreaded morning comes, the butterflies are rumbling in my tummy, and all I can think in my head is *I can't!*

Dad is in the kitchen, getting breakfast ready, and Mom is doing my hair. "Pigtail braids and a smile is all you need to succeed, Cannoli. You can do this. You can!"

Can Mom be right? Can I make new friends and learn new things? Can I do this? I take a deep breath in and slowly let it out. I put on my lucky pink dress, walk down the steps, and eat my french toast with Dad.

Before I know it, it is time to go. I grab my lunch box and matching purple backpack and walk slowly to the car. Mom has the camera, and Dad has the keys, and they are both singing a fun beat. "Cannoli can, Cannoli can. If anybody can, Cannoli can!"

Of course, I join in on the singing, and I have forgotten all about those nervous butterflies in my tummy. I have also forgotten all about the two words, "I can't!"

Dad pulls up to the front of the school and joins the long line of cars that have other families waiting for their turn to arrive. Teachers are greeting, students are skipping, and parents are snapping pictures, while their eyes are filled with joy.

This wasn't so bad. Cannoli, you can! I think to myself with pride. I hug Mom and Dad and take a deep breath, and the car door swings open wide. My teacher arrives with her arms stretched out, and the hug that she gives is so warm and tight. Why am I nervous? Why do I think this is not going to go right?

I've learned how to tie my shoes, I'm working on counting by twos, and my coloring is almost in the lines. I'm learning to cut, I can finally glue, and tomorrow I will begin to write. I've gained so many new friends, and I don't want this day to end. I can't wait for tomorrow to begin.

You can!

As we leave for dismissal, I start to whistle a tune that started the day off right, "Cannoli can, Cannoli can. If anybody can, Cannoli can!"

You can.

About the Author

Emily Jennings Dito was born and raised in Fort Worth, Texas. While she was growing up in Cowtown, her parents supported her in a variety of activities. One of those activities included summer reading programs through the local library. She developed a love for reading and writing during this young age, which led her to a dream of writing children's books of her own.

Emily attended Oklahoma Christian University in Edmond, Oklahoma. After graduating with a bachelor's degree in public relations, she returned to her home state of Texas. There she earned her Texas teaching certificate, and she is able to connect daily with children through laughter, stories, and the love of learning.

In her spare time, Emily enjoys spending time with her family and two dogs, Prim and Rue.

CPSIA information can be obtained
at www.ICGtesting.com
Printed in the USA
LVHW071033230822
726658LV00004B/99